KU-682-908

A Herbal

For Nicholas William

The letter in brackets after the botanical name of each herb refers to whether it is annual (A), biennial (B) or perennial (P). The figure suggests the approximate height to which the mature herb is likely to grow.

A Herbal

Reginald Peplow

Illustrated by Linda Garland
with line illustrations by Roger Garland

THE NATIONAL TRUST

UNWIN HYMAN
London Sydney

First published in Great Britain by Unwin Hyman,
Unwin Hyman Limited, 1987.

Published in asociation with The National Trust
for Places of Historic Interest or National Beauty.

© Reginald Peplow

© for illustrations Linda and Roger Garland 1987.

All rights reserved. No part of this publication
may be reproduced, stored in a retrieval system,
or transmitted in any form or by any means,
electronic, mechanical, photocopying, recording
or otherwise, without the prior permission of
Unwin Hyman Limited.

UNWIN HYMAN LIMITED
Denmark House, 37–39 Queen Elizabeth Street
London SE1 2QB
and
40 Museum Street
London WC1A ILU

Allen & Unwin Australia Pty Ltd
8 Napier Street, North Sydney, NSW 2060,
Australia

Allen & Unwin New Zealand Pty Ltd
with the Port Nicholson Press
60 Cambridge Terrace, Wellington, New Zealand

British Library Cataloguing in Publication Data
Peplow, Reginald
A herbal.
1. Herb gardening   2. Herbs
I. Title.   II. National Trust
635'.7   SB351.H5

ISBN 0–04–440048–9

Designed by **Elizabeth Palmer**
Typeset by **Latimer Trend & Company Ltd,
Plymouth**
Printed in Great Britain by
William Clowes Ltd, Beccles & London

Contents

Introduction

If you want a wonderful new interest, allowing you to forget melancholia forever, follow the example set by your ancestors and introduce herbs into your life.

There are hundreds of herbs which will not only do you good but which will help you transcend everyday cares.

As a start, buy a packet of marigold seeds from your local gardening shop. The photograph on the packet shows such promise, but what do you get inside? A few apparently dried up seeds looking as uninteresting as possible. Daylight robbery? Of course not, the seeds are your passports to pots full of colour if you follow the instructions.

Why not try it? When buying your seeds also buy a few pots with drainage holes and a bag of compost. Half fill the pots with the compost and lay a few seeds on the surface, close to each other but not touching. Cover them with half an inch of compost and stand the pots for about ten minutes in a few inches of water. Once the compost has had a good soaking, enclose each of the pots in a clear plastic bag and put them away out of direct light.

Within days tiny green leaves will appear. Remove the bags and stand the pots in the light. After about a week, when the leaves have grown stronger, stand the pots in tepid water to give the compost another soaking.

You've read all this before, but how often have you done it and given some thought to the process. The green leaves are bringing to fulfilment of the promise on the packet. Provided you continue watering and begin transplanting the seedlings into bigger pots, a window box, or the garden, there is every chance that the promise will be kept. At the end of the season you will be able to gather the seeds from the fading flower heads and have many more promises to sow in the future seasons or to give to your friends.

The promise doesn't end there. The growth period of the marigolds is interesting and the blooms themselves are most attractive. But the really rewarding and satisfying part is discovering how the plant can help you and others. Can you cook with it, turn it into a medicine, use it as an insect repellent? Here are some answers with a little history.

7

The virtues of marigold

Throughout the ages this humble sun-loving herb has been the standby of herbalists. Masquerading under many names, Jackanapes-on-Horseback was one of them, it has been employed for all purposes from pepping up cordials to easing the miseries of smallpox.

The Romans used marigold as a cure for warts. When the first settlers were leaving for what is now called America, they took marigold seeds with them to ensure a plentiful supply of the cottage garden flower they so cherished. They were well aware of the herb's many virtues including its ability to give relief from insect bites, boils, hard glands, frostbite, sprains, headaches and afflication of the ear, and its capacity as a wonderful yellow dye. In later years it was much used by both confederate and union forces in America to help control bleeding.

Most of the old herbals mention it, a 1699 volume stated that a conserve of marigolds and sugar 'cureth the trembling of the harte' while another suggested that the leaves would 'instantly give ease to any hot swellings'.

Henry VIII (of the six wives) sought in vain for the herb's aphrodisiac qualities but reported in his *Medycine of Pestilence* that a 'handful of marigolds' among other herbs would heal the sick person if taken before the dreaded pimples appeared.

When in 1577 Thomas Hyall in *The Gardener's Labrynth* claimed that marigold was a 'soveraigne remedy for the assuaging of the gravious pain of the teeth', the demand for the herb grew enormously.

The marigold, with other herbs, enjoyed a cure-all reputation, a fact noted by Rudyard Kipling:

> *Excellent herbs had our fathers of old,*
> *Excellent herbs to ease their pain,*
> *Alexanders and Marigold,*
> *Eyebright, Orris and Elecampane.*

But the fast-growing marigold's uses were not only for relieving life's little miseries, they added colour. The humble dyed their clothes with it while others, whom the priests said should have known better, tinted their hair.

Marigolds were much used as garlands for feasts and weddings, for the colouring of butter and cheese, as cordials and for adding colour to soups and other dishes. They seem to have been generally appreciated in this role though perhaps too much was not always a good thing. Charles Lamb, in his essay on Christ's Hospital, mentions that boiled beef was served on Thursdays 'with detestable marigolds floating in the pail to poison the broth'.

During the reign of Henry VII young men sent baskets of marigolds to the objects of their admiration on Lady Day and the compliment was returned by the ladies on St. Luke's Day. In fact, on this special day in some parts of the country young girls would infuse a handful of the flowers with some other herbs and sprinkle this over their bodies at bedtime in the certain knowledge that they would then dream of their true love. In other areas the girls would follow the man in question, dig up a little of the earth he had trod and plant this with marigold seed. They reasoned that as the plant grew, so would their sweetheart's love for them.

Marigolds also figured in Greek mythology. There is a story that Apollo, abiding on Mount Olympus, was so handsome that even the nymphs and shepherdesses

fought each other for his affections. Four little wood nymphs quarrelled over him so much that Apollo's sister, Diana, used her divine powers to quieten them by turning them into 'gold flowers'—the marigold of today.

Poets and writers through the centuries have been intrigued by the herb's delightful habit of 'closing down' for the night. Shakespeare, conscious of the heavy dews of the morning, observes in *The Winter's Tale:*

The marigold that goes to bed
*   wi' the sun,*
And with him rises weeping

This was also noticed by the lonely and abandoned King Charles I while imprisoned on the Isle of Wight. Before his trial, he wrote:

The marigold observes the Sun
More than my subjects me have
*   done.*

The plant's many common names have a bearing on this. One popular name was Mary's gold, derived from the observation that the herb was in bloom for all the festivals of the Virgin Mary. Other names were gold-bloom, Mary-bud, sun's gold and bees-love.

The Romans noted that the plant was usually in bloom on the first day of each month, the *calenda*, and from this derived its botanical name of *calendula*. As you will note from a later chapter, marigold also has an additional name of *officinalis* which indicates its ranking as an 'official' drug in the apothecaries' shops.

horehound

The marigold of today

Even in our scientific age the marigold still has much to offer. Its quick-healing virtues were noticed during the First World War when vast quantities of marigold flowers were shipped to France to make antiseptic. Tinctures of marigold, or infusions of fresh flowers, take the pain out of burns, scalds, insect bites and stings, and also arrest bleeding from knife wounds.

When infused in oil or incorporated in creams and lotions, the petals of marigold do wonders for inflamed skin conditions and act, as one writer put it, as 'a general tonic for the complexion'. Even warts, sprains, boils and painful menstruation are said by some experts to yield to extracts or lotions of marigold. In some country districts sufferers from varicose pains obtain relief from an astringent lotion made from soaking petals in witch hazel water.

Good cooks will tell you that chopped or whole petals can enliven cakes and buns and will decorate sweet and savoury dishes. The orange colour can readily be extracted from the petals to make a natural food colouring by simmering them in water

honeysuckle

or milk then liquidiing them in a blender. Fresh or dried petals add colour and flavour—some call it a delicate bitterness—to cheese dishes, salads, soups and omelettes. You can also make drinks and cordials from it, use it as a principal ingredient when concocting a custard or to season salads. Keep it in the greenhouse or among the beans as a natural white fly repellent.

It is amazing what a miserable little dried up seed can accomplish. If the common marigold can be so full of promise, what will you uncover when you probe the mysteries of the many other herbs you can grow from seed, buy as small plants in nurseries or even through the post? They all have their very special properties, and this book will help you to find some of them.

13

Agrimony

(Agrimonia eupatoria) (P) 50cm, 19in

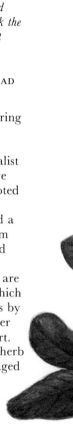

And here in handsome rows you can see my agrimony. It clothes the fields with its profusion; it grows wild in the woodland shade. If crushed and drunk the draught will check the most violent stomach ache.
WALAFRID STRABO
The Little Garden 840 AD

Often known as church steeples because of its tapering spires of small yellow blossoms, the herb was described by one old herbalist as 'good for them that have naughty livers' and was noted for the healing of wounds. Country folk made tea and a gargle for tired throats from the flowering tops and used the whole plant to make a yellow dye. The seed pods are armed with small hooks which become attached to passers by and animals hence the other country name of sticklewort. An attractive plant in the herb garden, it may be propagaged by seed or root division.

agrimony
alkanet
allspice

Alkanet

(Alkanna tinctoria) (B) 45cm, 17in

The funnel-shaped blue

alecost

flowers of the alkanet are often to be seen in bloom on ground where the plant can be mistaken for borage. There are several members of the alkanet tribe, all highly regarded in earlier times for the red colouring agent extracted from the thick roots used in the manufacture of pharmaceutical and cosmetic products, and by victuallers. Other names for alkanet are dyers bugloss and Spanish bugloss.

Alecost

(Chrysanthemum balsamita) (P) 60cm, 23in

As its name may suggest, this ancient herb was used in breweries, being particularly prized for giving a spicy flavour and soft balsamic odour to ale. It was also employed in the making of sweet washing water, taking the hurt out of bee stings and reducing the bitterness of spring salads. The plant's common name, bible leaf, stems from the New World when settlers used the long greyish green leaves to mark the places in the Bible.

15

Angelica

(Angelica archangelica) (B) 2m, 6ft

> *The whole plante, both leafe, roote and seede is of an excellent comfortable sent, savour and taste.*
>
> JOHN PARKINSON Paradisi in Sole 1629

This stately herb bears great green clusters of seed heads and exudes a dramatic musky aroma. Strictly speaking, the plant is a biennial but if the seed heads are removed, it will continue to grow for several years. Traditionally angelica was an antidote to the plague and the monks who ate it rarely suffered. When dried, the large green leaves are an excellent basis for pot pourri and make a relaxing tea. The stems may be cooked with rhubarb or soft fruits to give them a natural sweetness and gentle fragrance, and have been used by confectioners and bakers for centuries as sweetmeats.

Candied angelica

Cut the stems in the spring and slice them into 10cm, 4in pieces. Simmer in just enough water to cover until tender, strain and peel off the outer

16

skin. Return the pieces to the pan, add sufficient water to cover and bring to the boil. Strain, and when the pieces are cool weigh them and place in a covered dish with a similar weight of sugar. Leave in a cool place for two days to allow the angelica to absorb the sugar. Return the pieces to the pan (no water will need to be added) and allow to simmer until they become a good green colour. Strain, place the angelica on a plate and sprinkle lightly with sugar. Dry in a cool oven and store in an airtight jar.

Anise

(*Pimpinella anisum*) (A) 40cm, 15in

The small ridged seeds have a sweet aniseed taste which gives an appetising flavour and aroma to bread, cakes, biscuits, salads and vegetables, such as red cabbage. Small cakes containing the seed were offered to aid indigestion after Roman banquets, and the tradition of our own wedding cake may have originated here. When bruised the seeds make an excellent tea to aid indigestion; if honey is added the tea gives pleasant relief from a cold.

anise
lemon balm
basil

Bay

(Laurus nobilis) (**P**) bush

> *This Sweet Bay is the Laurel of the poets, of the first and greatest of all poet and artist nations of the earth—the laurel sacred to Apollo.*
> WILLIAM ROBINSON The English Flower Garden 1883

Our forefathers put bay leaves beneath their pillows to encourage inspiration as they slept. When they achieved distinction they decorated their heads with garlands of the herb. Today bay is used to flavour special dishes, repel insects, and as a decorative feature of the garden. Best regarded as an evergreen, aromatic shrub, bay is capable of taking on many shapes according to the whims of the gardener. It grows very slowly and prefers a warm, sheltered part of the garden. The shrub is susceptible to frost, and if growing outside, will need a netting cover as the weather gets colder. Bay will grow well in tubs and large pots, though frequent watering and some liquid feeding will be necessary. Bay 'trees' or 'mop heads' are bushes with all the lower stems and foliage

18

removed from the main stem. To keep the required shape, trimming and careful removal of new stem-growth and small shoots from the base must be done at least twice a year. An ideal place to stand a potted bush is by the kitchen door where the leaves can be picked fresh to give a delicate flavour to casseroles, pasta dishes, milk puddings and other culinary delights.

Borage

(*Borage officinalis*) (A) 60cm, 23in

Wine 'spiked' with the leaves and flowers of borage was a mediaeval remedy for melancholy, which no doubt fostered the adage 'I borage, bring always courage'. Today, the star-shaped gleaming blue flowers are still used to decorate wine cups and the cucumber-flavoured leaves give the summer fruit cup a kick no alcohol can emulate. Candy the flowers and use the leaves for salads. For a natural nightcap, inducing peaceful sleep, chop the leaves, and place in a tea pot or cup. Cover with boiling water, leave for a few minutes, strain and add a slice of lemon and a teaspoon of honey.

betony
borage

19

Box

(Buxus sempervirens) (P) up to 10m, 32ft

With wood as durable as brass and heavier than any other in Europe, this slow-growing evergreen with shiny green leaves was highly prized by wood engravers and makers of high quality chess sets. When the wood was cut, the sawdust was saved and sold to help dye greying hair. The dried and powdered leaves were given to horses to improve their coats and were an active ingredient in a once-renowned remedy for the bite of a mad dog. Box was used frequently as an edging to herb gardens. Trees were clipped into ornamental shapes, a practice called topiary, thought to have been originated with Emperor Julius Caesar.

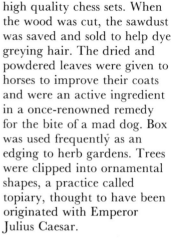

Broom

(Sarothamnus scoparius) (P) 2m, 6ft

This attractive shrub bears bright yellow flowers on twigs which were at one time used for besoms. A country name is Scotch broom. The botanical name means 'to sweep'. The seeds are useful as a coffee substitute. In former times the twig was useful to basket makers and the bark was

collected for use in the manufacture of clothes and paper. Broom yields a yellow dye but should not be confused with a similarly-named perennial, dyer's broom (*Genista tinctoria*). Also called dyer's greenwood, this yellow-flowered herb has no medicinal use but has for long been famous for its yellow green dye.

thunderstorms. The very large root could be shaped easily into the form of a man by making it grow in specially made moulds; these shapes were then sold as amulets, love charms and for protection against the Devil and the evil eye. All parts of the herb are poisonous, as are those of a similarly-named plant black bryony (*Tamus communis*), the berries of which can be fatal to children.

Bryony, White

(*Bryonia cretica subsp. dioica*)
climbing

A close relative of cucumbers, melons and marrows, this herb uses its tendrils to festoon our hedgerows and after the greenish flowers have gone it heralds winter's arrival with a mass of red berries. One of the herb's special claims to fame is that English herbalists used its twisting shape as shop signs, another is that Augustus Caesar wore a protective wreath of it during

Catmint

(Nepeta mussinii) (P) 30cm,
12in

Catmint was a vital
component in the medicine
chests of settlers in the New
World and is popular today as
a principal ingredient of
cough syrup. Blue-grey,
aromatic foliage and
lavender-blue flowers make an
attractive edging plant, much
loved by the bumble bee. It
needs protection from cats
who will roll on it and use it
as a personal sun-bed.

Catnip *(Nepeta cataria)* has
small white flowers and a
scented foliage also loved by
cats. Fresh and dried leaves
make a soothing tea which
was a staple brew in the
country before the import of
commercially grown tea. An
old herbalist reports however
that the root of the herb has
the power to make even the
most mild and agreeable
people wild and quarrelsome.

Propagation is by seed, root
division or cuttings. If cats are
a problem, follow the advice
of William Coles in his 1656
The Art of Simpling:

> *If you set it, the Catts will eate
> it,*
> *If you sow it, the Catts can't
> know it*

Sow seed instead of taking cuttings and take care to cover the seedlings with a net until they can take the force of a mature ginger cavorting among the aromatic leaves.

Celandine

(Ranunculus ficaria) (P) 1m, 3ft

The cheery star-like golden blossoms of the lesser celandine appear in late winter when there is little colour about. The poet

celandine
chamomile
chervil
chicory

Wordsworth loved them, and they are carved on his tomb. For all this, the happy little plant is poisonous when freshly picked and its only use in folk medicine has been in the treatment of piles. Greater celandine is more useful medicinally, for problems of the liver, and it had a reputation for restoring sight. The botanical name alludes to its habit of flowering when swallows began to arrive and fading during their migration.

Chamomile

(Chamaemelum nobile) (P) 30cm, 12in

Chamomile is called 'the plant's physician' due to the way it contributes to a healthy garden. Sickly plants often recover when the herb is grown near them, and many insect pests avoid areas where this pungent herb is plentiful. A herb of humility dedicated to St. Anne, this low-growing plant has a distinct aroma of ripe apples. Excellent tea may be brewed from the creamy, daisy-like flowers which is a relaxant and sedative. Each year, in early spring, the roots may be pulled apart to provide a dozen or so plants.

Chives

(Allium schoenoprasum) (**P**)
15cm, 6in

> *Cyves are used in meates and Pottages even as Leekes, which they do resemble in operation and vertue.*
>
> REMBERT DODOENS, A niewe Herball (trans.Lyte) 1578

When planted a few inches apart, chives make excellent edging and border plants. Their jolly lavender pom-pom flower heads attract bees and other winged insects. Chives grow well in a pot, and if kept by the kitchen door and well watered, will provide a supply of green stems with a most delicate onion flavour. To maintain quality, the clumps need to be broken up and replanted every two to three years. Cut the cylindrical, hollow leaves (called grass) with scissors frequently to provide strong growth. If looked after in this way, the herb will be at its best before other salad crops are ready and go on producing for many months. Unless needed for decoration, the flower heads should be removed as they open. Chop the grass to garnish and flavour mashed potatoes, egg dishes such as omelettes, salads, cottage cheese, grilled tomatoes and soups.

Clary

(Salvia sclarea) (P) 1m, 3ft

> *The seed is used to be put into the Eyes to cleer tham from Moats, or such like things gotten within the Lids to offend them, as also to cleer them from white or red spots on them.*
> NICHOLAS CULPEPER The English Physician Enlarged 1653

Clary wine, a potent aphrodisiac, made the herb famous in the sixteenth century. It was also used as a substitute for hops in the brewing of beer and reputedly made the drinker 'dead drunke, foolish drunke, or madde drunke'. Known also as clary sage and muscatel sage, the plant yields an oil used in flavouring and as a fixative in perfumery. The seeds were once turned into a concoction for cleansing the eye of grit and for drawing thorns out of the flesh; the powdered roots were taken as snuff to relieve headaches. Clary produces numerous attractive white, pink and blue flowers on bristly spires rising to five feet and its grapefruit-like fragrance is at its height on a warm summer evening after a shower of rain.

clary
coltsfoot
columbine

Comfrey

(Symphytum officinale) (P) 1m, 3ft

> *The slimie substance of the roote made in a posset of ale, and given to drinke against the paine in the back, gotten by any violent motion, as wrestling, or overmuch use of women, doth in fower or five daies perfectly cure the same . . .*
>
> JOHN GERARD The Herball 1597

An untidy, vigorous plant which has a firm place in both herbal folk lore and modern medicine. Comfrey has rough and hairy leaves and bell-shaped flowers which vary in colour from cream to light blue. Long regarded as the gardener's friend and physician, it has numerous cures accredited to it. In the past, the leaves of the plant were used as a salve for mending broken bones, hence its country name 'old knitbone'. Today, beaten and warmed comfrey leaves can be applied as a soothing and anti-inflammatory poultice to cuts, boils, burns and abscesses. Dried roots of the herb, powdered and dissolved in water to form a mucilage will also treat bruises, sprains and insect bites.

Comfrey is easily propagated from root cuttings and prefers open ground where its extensive root grows deep to tap essential minerals and moisture. The large leaves make valuable potash-rich compost.

To make comfrey ointment for insect bites and to help cuts and grazes heal quickly, spoon the contents of an 8oz jar of petroleum jelly into a small bowl in a saucepan of boiling water. Add a handful of freshly picked and chopped Comfrey leaves to the jelly

important ingredient of alcoholic drinks and has for long been used to disguise the unpleasant taste of medicine.

coriander
cowslip
cuckoopint

and let the water simmer for 20 minutes. Strain the liquid ointment through a piece of muslin and pour into a container with a tight-fitting lid and when cool store in a refrigerator.

Coriander

(Coriandrum sativum) (A) 70cm, 27in

Known as Chinese parsley, where the plant was thought to have the power of bestowing immortality, coriander is grown more for its aromatic seeds than for the bright green and feathery leaves. The sandy, ridged seeds have many uses as a spicy flavouring for meats, curries, cheeses, salads, soup and bread. Coriander seeds formed according to legend, the biblical manna from Heaven, lifted from its husks by a passing wind, and the best still comes from the Middle East where it has been cultivated for more than three thousand years. It is also an

27

Dandelion

(Taraxacum officinale) (**P**)
30cm, 12in

Every part of the much
maligned dandelion is useful
and although the plant is a
nuisance in the lawn it
deserves a place in the
vegetable garden or in a deep
pot by the back door. The
succulent jagged-edged leaves
can be picked and used fresh
in spring as an addition to
salads. They are considered to
be as good for the system as
spinach and are particularly
tasty when crisped–up by a
short spell in the refrigerator.
The slightly bitter taste of
older leaves can be
counteracted by dipping them
for a minute in boiling water
and then refreshing them
under a cold tap. The leaves,
dried or fresh, make an
uplifting tea. Home wine
makers understand the virtues
of the golden flowers. Health
addicts who dislike
supermarket coffee make their
own brew using the roasted
and ground up root.
Dandelion beer and stout

remains a popular drink in some areas.

Herbalists of both past and present stress the value of what has, alas, become a weed to most of us. All parts of the herb, including the root, are used in medicine for combating rheumatism, chronic skin complaints and disorders of the digestion, liver and gall bladder. Eaten raw it stimulates the appetite and acts as a mild laxative.

Dill

(Anethum graveolens) (A) 1m, 3ft

The seeds be chiefly occupied in medicine, and of the greene herbs Galen writeth that it procureth sleepe. Wherefore in olde time they used to weare garlands of dill at their feasts.
THOMAS COGHAN The Haven of Health 1584

An ancient drug used for centuries to charm the wind out of babies and to help magicians with their spells, dill's lace-like foliage and umbels of dainty, bright yellow flowers delight flower arrangers, while the seeds are of great culinary use. Often mistaken for fennel, but not as boisterous in growth, dill is equally happy in a pot or in a window-box, as in the garden. To maintain supplies, sow small quantities of seeds in late spring and throughout the summer. A few twigs pushed into the soil will provide support without spoiling the shape of the plant. Leaves, sometimes termed dillweed, should be picked fresh, but the seed is best collected when just ripe and used when dry. Dill leaves and seeds are used increasingly for flavouring fish, potato and many other dishes, and for pickling, making vinegar, sauces and dressings. A tisane made from a teaspoon of seed and a teaspoon of honey is an excellent aid to digestion and relieves hiccups.

Elder

(Sambucus nigra) (P) bush tree

So many superstitions and beliefs surround elder that it has never been truly popular in the kitchen, but it is booty for the brave-of-heart with time to dip into old and new cookery books. Flowerheads, for example, if tied in a muslin bag and cooked with gooseberries give a delicious muscat flavour to the dish. They can also be turned into a wonderful fizzy non-alcoholic summer drink, an ointment for insect bites and chapped hands, and a lotion for freshening the skin and disguising freckles. Elderberry wine made from the ripe berries is renowned.

Early summer is the best time to pick the flower heads. To dry them, spread them on old material in a tray and keep them warm but well-ventilated until papery to the touch. The berries are ready for picking when they have turned shiny and purple.

The hollow stems of elder were used for blowing up a fire, and it has been argued that 'the shrillest pipes and most sonorous horns' were made from elder 'grown out of the reach of cock-crow'.

Several English proverbs suggest that summer is not here until the elder bush displays its clusters of creamy white flowers and ends when the berries are ripe. The fine grain of the wood led to elder being used for butchers skewers, for combs and for instruments, yet the wood is renown for its hardness. Fixed to doors on the last day of April, it is said, to keep witches at bay. The herb's medicinal qualities were summed up by one herbalist who declared it was 'the medicine chest of the country people' and 'a whole magazine of physic to rustic practitioners'. He raised his hat every time he passed a bush. Elder was a panacea for every malady from simple toothache to the plague and was said to stride a man's life-time, helping him into the world, making love potions and finally seeing him out when the drivers of hearses used elderwood whips.

Elecampane

(Inula helenium) (P) 2–3m, 6–9ft

Elecampane was eaten as vegetable in ancient Rome,

but more recently monks used it as a remedy for chest disorders brought on by spartan monastic life. This tall, attractive plant with its great yellow flower heads may still be found around old monasteries. The monks made an infusion of the roots using sugar, currants and white port, and drank this as a sweet cordial. Also called scabwort, a reference to its alleged power to cure skin diseases, it was used extensively in stables and sheepfolds. The herb's root was much prized as a sweetmeat and was sold in London as flat round cakes until the late 1920s. The costermongers (market salesmen who sold costard apples in mediaeval times) declared that a piece sucked, when travelling up the Thames was a safeguard against bad air.

Eyebright

(Euphrasia rostkoviana) (A)
30cm, 12in

This elegant little plant with what looks like a bloodshot eye is semi–parasite, needing the company of other roots. It is used in herbal smoking mixtures and as a mild eye lotion. Tradition has it that linnets use the herb for cleaning the eyes of their young. But it will treat head colds and can be used as a poultice.

Fennel

(Foeniculum vulgare) 2–3m,
6–8ft (P)

> *I have pepper and paeony seed
> and a pound of garlick, And a
> farthingworth of fennel-seed, for
> fasting days.*
> WILLIAM LANGLAND Piers
> Plowman 1377

> *Decorative and useful, the
> sun-loving Green Fennel, also
> called Sweet Fennel, seems to
> explode each year almost
> overnight to form an attractive
> clump of aromatic feathers. The
> seeds contain a high
> concentration of volatile oil
> which our forefathers used to
> help clear mistiness of the eye
> and, so the old herbalists
> reported, to drive worms out of
> their ears.*

> *Both the seeds, leaves and roots
> . . . are much used in drinks and
> broths for those that are grown
> fat; to abate their unwieldiness
> and cause them to grow more
> gaunt and lank.*
> WILLIAM COLES The Art of
> Simpling 1656

Slimmers appreciate a tea
made from fennel seeds, as it
quietens hunger pangs and
soothes the stomach. For
cooks, a fresh supply of green
fennel leaves is essential as an
aromatic stuffing and
decoration for fish dishes or
eaten raw in salads. A
decorative variety of fennel
has a mass of velvet textured
bronze leaves and makes an
attractive garden plant.
Florence fennel is less
attractive, but appeals to
cooks because of its white
bulbous base root, with crisp
texture and delicate aniseed
flavour.

Fennel was cultivated by
the Romans as a vegetable,
and was thought then to have
the power to restore vision.
Herbalists declared that
serpents 'sharpen their sight
with the juice by rubbing
against the plant'. The herb
was hung over doors on
Midsummer's eve to ward off
evil spirits and used as a
condiment to the salt fish
eaten during Lent. Fennel is
propagated from seed.

Fenugreek

(Trigonella foenum-graecum) (A)
40cm, 15in

The herb's outlandish name is
an abbrevation of its botanical
name, which means Greek
hay. It has been in use for
centuries as a fodder crop and
later found by the Benedictine

monks to be a valuable vegetable and to yield a yellow dye. The celery flavoured seeds can be roasted and drunk as a coffee and are used to spice curry and flavour chutney. The fresh leaves, shaped like red clover, are a useful tonic if infused.

Feverfew

(Chrysanthemum parthenium) (P)
75cm, 29in

Since Shakespeare's day, people suffering from serious headaches have been given relief by eating the leaves of this attractive wild plant. Herbalists of the time recorded the beneficial effects of a 'daily dose' of feverfew and apart from prescribing it for headaches, also used it for relief of 'swimming of the head' and for aching bones. Now, after many years of neglect, the plant has come

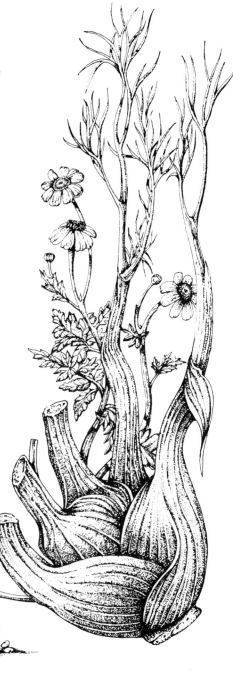

into its own again. Serious clinical trials are still taking place but there is little doubt that feverfew is winning a place in medical history.

Feverfew is an attractive garden plant throwing out feathery leaves and bright white single and double daisy-like flowers. It can be propagated very easily from seed or cuttings and grows well in any soil but seems to produce the best leaves when in a semi-shady position. A good plan is to have a couple of plants indoors on a window-sill (not the kitchen, where extremes of heat will affect its growth) and four outside in the garden or in pots. Allow one plant to flower so that the seeds may be kept for friends. Feverfew may also be planted among broad and runner beans as a natural deterrent to beanfly.

Flax

(Linum usitatissimum) (P)
50cm, 20in

The lovely blue-flowering flax has been in the service of man for the last five thousand years. Seeds, known as linseed, and woven cloth found in ancient Egyptian tombs point to flax as being the source of the 'fine linen' of the Bible. Flax was harvested, beaten and woven for white sails, lamp wicks, fishnets, ropes, thread, bowstrings, bed linen, sacks, bags and purses. Today, we use the larger seeds of the commercially grown flax for oil and for cattle feeds but the small ones can still be grown and make ideal snacks for the birds.

Foxglove

(*Digitalis purpurea*) (B) 1.5m, 5ft

When in 1785, a Dr William Withering told the world that this stately though common herb could have a desirable effect on a weak heart, the value of the plants as a source of medicine increased enormously and has continued to do so. Until Dr Withering's discovery, respect for the properties of foxglove was on the decline. It was thought to be a 'violent medicine', too strong for use even as far back as 1542, when its botanical name was coined in reference to the finger-like shape of the attractive purple flowers. According to superstition, the herb was named foxglove after elves fitted the bell-shaped flowers much loved by bees to a vixen's feet so that she could walk silently through the fields and not disturb their slumbers. Many varieties exist for garden ornamentation. The plant may be propagated by seed.

Foxglove is still cultivated commercially for its medicinal properties and as an external poultice to aid healing of wounds. It is a poisonous plant and should not be used for medical purposes by the lay person.

35

Garlic

(Allium sativum) (P) 40cm, 15in

Roman soldiers ate the cloves raw to sustain them on long marches, to cleanse the system and to improve the circulation. A member of the onion tribe, it has plenty of uses in the kitchen and home medicine chest. Crushed cloves are the basis of several popular and effective cold cures, and when mixed with petroleum jelly as an ointment can bring relief to rheumatic pain. A belief that a garlic clove sliced and worn inside a sock will prevent a cold and help rheumatics is popular but not proven; also not proven is a theory that a bald man can bring back hair by rubbing his scalp with a sliced clove.

Garlic is easy to grow and as an insect deterrent has few equals. Grown under a peach tree, it will prevent curly leaf and mitigate other problems with the fruit.

Garlic can be readily purchased and the bulbs should be split into individual cloves for planting. Place just below soil level, about 25cm, 8in apart in the first two months of the year. A good warm summer will produce a healthy crop which can be dug up in the autumn and strung up to dry in a warm, shady place.

Gentian

(Gentiana lutea) (P) 70cm, 27in

Gentius, King of Illyria, who died nearly two thousand

years before Christ, introduced this yellow–flowered alpine herb to medicine and its thick taproot has been regarded through the centuries as the most bitter plant material known. An effective appetiser, it is used to add the necessary bitter flavour to a number of alcoholic drinks. The erect stems reach a surprising height, making it an attractive long-lived garden plant.

Geranium

(Geranium robertianum) (A)
50cm, 20in

The geranium herb robert, also called red robin, is an unpleasant smelling, small herb which, according to legend was considered noxious until one of the founders of the Cistercian order of monks used it to treat patients suffering from plague-like illnesses. A wild plant, it is still used in folk medicine as an eyewash. More pleasing to the eye, palate and nostril are other geraniums and pelargoniums whose aromatic leaves are a source of great delight.

germander
goat's beard
Good King Henry

Ground Elder

(Aegopodium podagraria) (P)
30cm, 12in

One of the many herbs used by monks to heal the sick, this creeping herb is also called herb gerard and bishops weed in recognition of Gerard, the saintly man who used it to help relieve painful gout. It has many other country names, including goutweed. The herb has for centuries been a nuisance in orchards and gardens and difficult to eradicate. It produces large umbels of small white flowers followed by seeds which pop to a distance in the wind, hence a local name Jack-jump-about.

Ground Ivy

(Glechoma hederacea) (P) 20cm, 20in

A very old and popular remedy for inflamed eyes, this low growing herb was much used by brewers to clarify ale and to improve its flavour and keeping qualities. A country name is Gill-over-the-ground, and Gill tea made from the strong-smelling leaves is regarded as a good tonic and stomach settler. The dark green kidney-shaped leaves and long lasting blushes of purplish flowers are attractive and the fast-growing virtually evergreen plant is becoming popular as ground cover.

Groundsel

(Senecio vulgaris) (A) 40cm, 15in

The yellow flower heads are gathered by bird fanciers, now the only friends of this once popular herb. The herb's name derives from old English and means ground swallower, a term with which most gardeners would agree. At one

groundsel

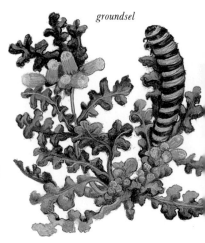

time groundsel was used to treat forms of illness caused by 'heat'. It was later used for liver diseases but found not to be effective. The herb followed civilized man everywhere, probably because its seeds mixed with grain. In folklore, it was considered that the roots dug out of the ground with a wooden spade (not iron) and then smelled would cure headaches and if fed to horses would help expel worms. In the Fens, potato pickers still bathe their chapped hands in a warm tea made with the herb.

Hawthorn

(Crataegus monogyna) (P) bush.

Henry VII chose the bush as his heraldic device after the battle of Bosworth, when a small crown from Richard's helmet was found hanging from a hawthorn branch. It is regarded as a sacred herb, for it furnished the crown of thorns. At Glastonbury there is a thornless hawthorn with deep religious connections, which supposedly blooms once a year at Christmas. It is not a pleasant smelling herb and traditionally still carries the

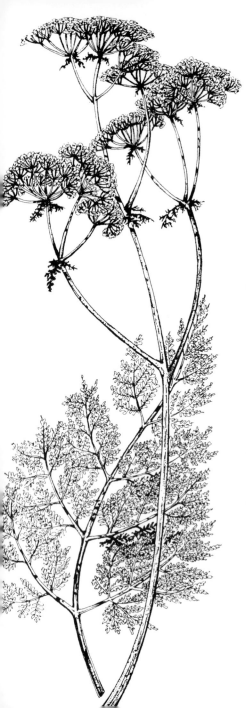

aroma of the Great Plague of London. Its fine-grained wood is much prized by craftsmen for its superb polishing qualities. Hawthorn is first class stock for grafting and the wood makes the hottest fire and best charcoal.

Hemlock

(Conium maculatum) (P) 1m, 3ft

Juice extracted from roots is deadly to humans and filled the notorious hemlock cup of ancient Athens which the philosopher Socrates was forced to drink. In mediaeval times, the juice was added at the rate of one drop a day to a piece of sweet pastry as a preventive against cholera, a remedy for hernia, epilepsy and pleurisy, and a tonic. Today, the dried unripe fruit of poisonous hemlock is used as a powerful narcotic sedative.

Henbane

(Hyoscyamus niger) (A) 80cm, 31in

And old herb, much used in Elizabethan times to procure

sleep and allay pains, this deadly member of the nightshade family has a sticky stem and nauseating odour. Its name is derived from the Anglo-Saxon for chicken murderer, because when fowls eat the seeds they become paralyzed and die. Its medical history is lengthy, and despite its poisonous nature it has been employed as a love potion. Juice has been used as an anti-spasmodic for conditions of asthma and whooping cough and as a mouthwash tea for toothache. In some areas an oil from the herb or a poultice from the hairy leaves is applied to relieve pains in the joints.

Hollyhock

(*Althaea rosea*) (B) 2m, 6ft

When it was first brought
from China in the 16th
century, this well known
garden plant was boiled with
other pot herbs and regarded
as a great delicacy. It was also
used as a medicine particularly
as a tea for chest complaints.
The flowers, varying in colour
from yellow to purple, gained
popularity as a colouring for
wine. The plant is easily raised
from seed.

Honeysuckle

(*Lonicera periclymenum*) (P) 6m,
20ft

I know bank where the wild

Hops

thyme blows,
Where oxlips and the nodding
*   violet grows*
Quite overcanopied with luscious
*   woodbine,*
With sweet musk-roses and with
*   eglantine*
A Midsummer Night's
Dream

A true plant of midsummer,
the herb is also called
woodbine because of the way
it hugs the trunks of trees. It
was much used in Elizabethan
times to provide shady hiding
places for lovers.
Traditionally, honeysuckle was
grown up posts at entrances to
herb gardens so that the
trailing stems could brush
witches and devils from the
backs of all visitors. It was,
and remains, a favourite plant
in cottage gardens and is
easily propagated from woody
cuttings taken in early
autumn.

(Humulus lupulus) (P) climbing

Hops are now a declining
crop, but a golden variety is
available and if grown up
sticks to form a wigwam can
add height and interest to a
garden. The Romans
cultivated the crop as a
garden herb and through the
centuries the young tips have
been eaten as a salad
vegetable. Of course, the herb
is best known in brewing. In
Henry VIII's day, petitioners
claimed that the herb was 'a
wicked weed that would spoil
the taste of the drink and
endanger the people'; this
followed its introduction from
Bavaria as a replacement for
alecost and other traditional
bitter herbs. Hops are used in
sleep pillows and the leaves
make a pleasant tea.
Propagation is from cuttings
in early summer.

43

Horehound

(Marrubium vulgare) (P) 60cm,
24in

A downy plant, others call it
woolly, horehound is best
known as a delicious candy
sucked to alleviate the miseries
of coughs and colds. It has
been used as a cough remedy
for centuries and the fresh
green leaves with sugar make
a delicious syrup to ease a sore
throat. It was one of the bitter
herbs the Jews were ordered to
take for the Feast of the
Passover and a principal
ingredient of Caesar's antidote
to vegetable poisons. Few
European immigrants left the
land of their birth without
seeds and roots of horehound
in their baggage, so the herb
flourishes in America, Canada
and many other countries.
Propagation is by root division
and seed sown in late spring.

Horseradish

(Cochlearia armoracia) (P) 1m,
3ft

There are many who will
agree with the herbalist who
wrote in 1640 that a sauce
made from the root of this

horehound
horseradish
houseleek

well-known herb is 'too strong for tender and gentle stomachs' and more suitable for 'strong labouring men'. On the other hand, horseradish is a taste which, once acquired, 'brings solace and delight'. As a compliment to beef, fish and poultry, it has long been renowned as an excellent stimulant and aid to the digestive organs. The large coarse green leaves are to be found alongside many roads. The plant grows with great vigour and may be propagated by planting a small section of root or sowing seeds in early spring.

Houseleek

(Sempervivum tectorum) (P) 12cm, 4in

The leaning flower stems of this strange cactus-like herb may be responsible for the delightful country name welcome–home–husband however–drunk–ye–be. Little is known about it, ancient though it is, but records show that the large rosettes of fleshy leaves were grown on houseroofs and barns for centuries, mainly to guard the property against fire and lightening. The bruised leaves were applied as a poultice to give quick relief from burns, scalds and grazes; warts and corns were charmed away by rubbing them with a cut leaf of the plant. Houseleeks need little or no attention, and a leaf tucked under a tile or into a wall crevice will usually grow and multiply in the most rewarding fashion.

Hyssop

(Hyssopus officinalis) (P) 50cm, 20in

> *Purge me with Hyssop and I*
> *   shall be clean;*
> *Wash me, and I shall be whiter*
> *   than snow.*
> Psalms 51,7

This highly scented herb was formerly as much prized for improving the 'tone' of a delicate stomach as for strewing on the floors of the great houses. Hyssop has a place in the kitchen, but use with discretion as the leaves are very pungent. A single chopped leaf in a stuffing mixture is sufficient. Tea made from the leaf brings relief to coughs and colds. While salad made with fresh green tops was once popular for the relief of rheumatism. A very fine oil is produced from leaf, stem and flower.

It is a neat plant with rich blue flowers throughout the summer. Although it has a natural preference for a sunny, sheltered corner, it is an ideal border plant, remaining evergreen except in the hardest winters. Propagate by root division.

Jacob's Ladder

(Polemonium caeruleum) (P) 50cm, 20in

The ladder–like shape of the leaves accounts for the name of this herb. It is much loved by cats, who will seek it out and roll on it. The herb has attractive spikes of blue flowers and light green leaves, which makes it an interesting addition to the herb garden or border, but its days of use in folk medicine are gone. It was formerly used to abate fevers and relieve nervous complaints and was supposed to have special powers to treat rabies. Propagation is by root division and seed sown in the spring.

Jasmine

(Jasminum officinale) (P) 5m, 16ft

The fragrant common white jasmine is a highly esteemed climber which often reaches a great height when supported and is still grown with other climbing herbs to provide shade. As the flowers come mainly from the young shoots, the plant needs severe pruning if the full fragrance is to be enjoyed. From this has been selected what is known as the

Jacob's ladder
jasmin
juniper

46

Catalonian jasmine with its delicately sweet odour. The old herbalists included jasmine in their potions to help those who were overburdened with toil and worry. But they knew, as do modern practitioners and perfumers, that the oil from the herb is among the world's most powerful stimulants. It is highly valued by the perfumery industry, where it is known as *Grasse*.

Juniper

(Juniperus communis) (P) 6m, 19ft

The berries of the common juniper, a hardy evergreen,

lady's mantle

take three months to ripen but when they are bluish-black in colour they should be harvested and used while fresh. Apart from flavouring gin, they also add a special taste to marinades and meat dishes, and are an important ingredient in sauerkraut and spiced beef. Health enthusiasts chew the fresh berries to cleanse the system or make tea from them as a tonic.

If you have juniper growing wild in your area, there is no point in cultivating a bush. They are, however, attractive features in a garden and keep their colour during the winter. Extract the seed from ripe berries and sow these at once in pots under cover. When the seedlings are an inch high, transplant them into individual pots and plant them into their growing position two years later.

Lady's Mantle

(Alchemilla mollis) (P) 30cm, 12ins

For an inexplicable reason this herb was most favoured by classical writers whose belief in its magical properties could not be shaken. It was held in awe through the centuries and

48

even today the botanical name meaning 'little magical one' is retained. Perhaps this is due to the shape of the leaf which, apart from looking like a lady's cloak is so formed that it holds the morning dew for hours after moisture has evaporated elsewhere. Our forefathers considered dew to be strongly magical, so the herb was treated accordingly. The leaves were put on to sores to dry them out and abate inflammation. It is a very attractive plant, the 'lion's foot' bright green leaves and haze of yellow flowers brighten any place where it is grown. It is best propagated by root division in autumn and requires a well watered position.

Lavender

(Lavandula angustifolia) (P) 50cm, 20in

It is generally known that the Queen (Victoria) is a great believer in Lavender as a disinfectant, and that she is not at all singular in her faith in this plant . . . The royal residences are strongly impregnated with the refreshing odour of this old fashioned flower, and there is no perfume that the Queen likes better than Lavender-water, which, together with the oil for disinfecting purposes, Her Majesty has direct from a lady who distils it herself.

DONALD McDONALD
Fragrant Flowers 1895

There are many varieties of the herb but the silver-grey foliage and long flowering heads of English lavender make it the most popular and useful. The other varieties are well worth investigating as the subtleties of colouring, size and shape fulfill most gardener's whims. The herb is best propagated by taking cuttings in late summer when the wood is half ripe. Mature bushes should be cut right back after flowering to encourage new growth. Lavender spikes should be cut when in full flower, taking as much of the stem as possible. Tie the stalks into convenient bunches, plunge head first into paper bags and hang them in a warm, well ventilated place to dry. The uses of dried lavender are many.

lavender

Lemon Verbena

(Aloysia triphylla) (P) 2m, 6ft

Lemon Verbena has many uses. The leaves are an important addition to pot pourri and the aroma from newly bruised leaves induces sleep. A single leaf will impart a gentle lemony fragrance to a cake or rice dish and a leaf or two may also be used to enhance wine and other drinks. A leaf in a trouser or jacket pocket will stay fragrant for weeks and several can be left in a car to counteract tobacco smoke and other smells. Moths and other insects dislike the lemon scent, so the leaves are useful in drawers, airing cupboards and among garments stored in wardrobes.

In the garden, lemon verbena is an attractive bush as it releases its superb perfume into the air when touched or brushed against. If left outside, it needs protection against frost. Cuttings can be taken in the autumn and brought on indoors as a precaution against the weather. As a house plant, it grows well if given plenty of light and freedom from draughts. When it is at rest during the winter it resembles a wooden stick but it will spring into new and vigorous life as the weather gets warmer. Propagation is from cuttings in spring and summer.

Lily of the Valley

(Convallaria majalis) (P) 15cm, 6in

This herb became popular for its medicinal qualities comparatively recently. The flowering shoots are important in some countries as an ingredient of drugs regulating the action of the heart. The fragrance, employed by perfumers, is slight, but it was thought to draw the nightingale into the glade in search of a mate. An old Sussex legend relates that St Leonard did combat with a marauding dragon in the forest now named after him. The saint received severe wounds, and wherever his blood fell, lilies of the valley sprang up—probably a reference to the scarlet fruit of the herb.

The herb was a useful flavouring agent for beers and tobacco. Propagation is by root division and its preferred position is in a shady recess.

51

Liquorice

(*Glycyrrhiza glabra*) (P) 1.2m,
4ft

Below ground there is an
extensive net-work of roots
and underground stems, which
have considerable commercial
value. These run out from the
main plant for up to 9m, 30ft,
sending up shoots which grow
into new plants. The herb was
introduced to Pontefract by
the black friars, but today all
the root is imported. The
sweet taste of the root is a
substance called glycyrrhizin,
which is fifty times sweeter
than sugar and best known as
a confection. An extract is
used medicinally in cough and
throat lozenges, as an
antispasmodic for intestine
and stomach muscles, and for
the treatment of stomach
ulcers.

Lobelia

(*Lobelia inflata*) (P) 30cm,
12ins

Lobelia is more often referred
to as Indian tobacco, since the
plant's pale blue leaves were
smoked by North American
Indians as a stimulant and to
relieve respiratory problems

such as asthma. It was used
for this purpose until the late
seventeenth century when the
herb's poisonous properties
were recognized. In a famous
court case of the time, a well
known herbal doctor was
charged with murder after a
patient died while taking it.
Settlers in the New World
considered it a panacea and
the plant was cultivated on a
large scale. Now the hairy,
erect great lobelia (*L.
siphilitica*) is a popular garden
plant, and it's blue and mauve
flowers provide much pleasure
in the warm days of summer.

Lungwort

(*Pulmonaria officinalis*) (P)
40cm, 15in

According to the so-called
Doctrine of Signatures it was
originally thought that a
medicinal herb, or 'simple' as
it was called then, should look
or behave like the organ or
illness it was intended to cure.
Lungwort is a good example
of this theory. A feature of
this creeping plant is the long
narrow leaf which is spotted
with white and resembles what
was imagined to be the
appearance of a diseased lung.
Hence the name lungwort

lovage

(wort means herb), and the botanical name, which indicates the herb's use for pulmonary problems. The herb is interesting also because the colours of the small flowers change quickly from pink to blue which might also account for the other country name, soldiers and sailors, which alluded to the colour of their uniforms. It makes good ground cover beneath trees and bushes.

Lovage

(Levisticun officinale) (P) 2m, 6ft

Not unlike celery in appearance and taste, lovage is a handsome garden plant and although somewhat neglected, is well worth growing for its dark green leaves, stems and seeds all of which can be used in the kitchen and the bathroom. Rich in vitamins, the leaves are ideal in small quantities for flavouring and garnishing and are an excellent addition to salads, soups, casseroles and stews. Its flavour is described as a cross between celery and yeast. The stems can be candied as sweetmeats and cake decorations, while the

53

seeds should be sprinkled on home-made bread and biscuits. The Romans appreciated the deodorant qualities of lovage and used it in their private and public bathing places. This practice can be followed by putting some of the dried leaves in a muslin bag, tying this to the bath taps and letting the hot water run through it. Propagation is by seed, or root division.

Madder

(Rubia tinctorum) (P) 75cm, 30in

The brilliant red of cardinal's cloaks and those of other dignatories through the centuries was produced with a dye made from the powdered and partially fermented roots of this little-known climbing herb. Other colours it yields are purple, orange and yellow. Madder gave its name to maddering, one of the final processes of cloth making. The leaf clusters were once gathered for polishing metalwork. The root was valued in the treatment of stomach disorders and for dyeing bones and urine in medical work. When staked,

the plant will grow to a height of 2.5m, 8ft but the prickly stalks often fall short and lie along the ground.

Mallow

(Malva sylvestris) (P) 85cm, 33in

An attractive plant and not unlike an enlarged pink flowered geranium in some respects, the common mallow was popular in Roman times as a vegetable for the table and was thought also to purge the system very gently of disease. The large, grey, downy and heart-shaped leaves are beautifully soft and were used medicinally to soothe inflammation, while the roots were a treatment for chest complaints. Mallow derives from the latin word malva for soft, referring to the leaves. There are several members of the mallow family, the most popular now being Marshmallow (*Althaea officinalis*), which reaches 1m, 3ft in height and is an attractive garden plant. This mallow has many properties valuable for the relief of chest complaints. Propagation is by seed or division of the fleshy tap roots with a sharp knife.

Mandrake

(Mandragora officinarum) (P)
30cm, 12in

Herbs which are imbued with superstition and folklore are particularly special. Most are pretty and loving, like heartsease. Others are evil, or would seem to be so, and the most repellent of them all is mandrake. Harmful properties have been attributed to the herb and it has been the subject of various magical rites designed to increase the importance and the wealth of the medicine men of the day. Romans and Greeks used mandrake as an anaesthetic but in later years apothecaries and cure mongers wielded it as an instrument of fear, aided by the fact that the shape of the root resembled the human form. They fostered the belief that anyone digging up the tuber would die, and so it became necessary to tie a dog to the plant and uproot it in this way. A feature of mandrake is the smooth-skinned orange fruit which lie close to the ground like a clutch of monster's eggs. This dangerous, poisonous and decidedly odd-looking herb is rare nowadays and much cherished by collectors who do

have a plant. It is worth seeking out, but if you are superstitious keep your distance.

Marigold

(Calendula officinalis) (A) 70cm, 27ins

The single golden flowers of the herb have delighted cottagers and poets for centuries. Fresh and dried petals flavoured soups, syrups and conserves. (For more about the marigold see introduction.

Marigold buns
Buns made with marigold petals are delicious and colourful. Cream together 4oz (100g) of margarine and the same quantity of sugar. Add two beaten eggs and mix in 6oz (150g) of self-raising flour. Mix in 3 tablespoons (3 × 15ml spoons) of marigold petals. Fill papercases three quarters full with the mixture and bake in a moderate oven for 15 minutes.

Marjoram

(Origanum majorana) (P) 30cm, 12in

> *The Sweet Marieromes are not onely much used to please the outward senses in nosegays, and in the windowes of houses, as also in sweete powders, sweete bags, and sweete washing waters, but are also of much use in Physicke, both to comfort the outward members, or parts of the body, and the inward also*
> JOHN PARKINSON Paradisi in Sole 1629

Cooks keen to grow marjoram for its warming, spicy flavour will usually select this sweet knotted annual, which, grown in our climate, gives a subtle flavour. Pot marjoram *(Origanum onites)*, also called oregano, is closely related. It has the stronger flavour of the two and is more suited to Greek and Italian dishes. Marjoram prefers a sunny position and flourishes in pots and window boxes. It may be started from seed though pot marjoram can be increased by root division. The leaves can be used fresh or dried. To dry them, cut the stems halfway down and hang them in a bunch from a hook in the kitchen. It is convenient to take a sprig from the bunch and crumble the leaves as needed. Apart from flavouring dishes, marjoram can be used as a tranquillising tea in times of stress and as a comforting bath mixture. In Elizabethan times marjoram was strewn over floors to keep them smelling sweet and was a popular ingredient of many dishes. *In All's Well That Ends Well*, Shakespeare writes of good gentlewomen who were 'the sweet marjoram of the salad'.

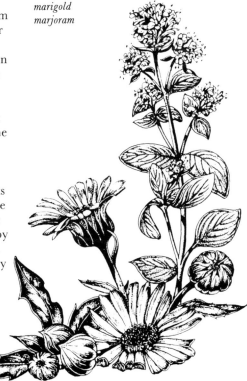

marigold
marjoram

meadowsweet

Meadowsweet

(Filipendula ulmaria) (P) 1m, 3ft

> *Queen Elizabeth of famous memorie did more desire meadowsweet than any other sweete herbe to strewe her chambers withall*
> JOHN PARKINSON 1640

Here, indeed, is a good recommendation for this elegant, fragrant herb, whose country name is queen of the meadow. Meadowsweet could once be seen dominating damp meadowland, standing almost to the jaw bones of the cattle but it is now, sadly, a rare sight. The herb was used to flavour and sweeten many types of beers and wine cups, particularly Elizabethan mead. It has an important place in medicinal history as it was in the flower buds that salicylic acid was first discovered in 1839, which led to the production of aspirin.

Melilot

(Melilotus officinalis) (B) 1m, 3ft

Invaluable in folk and commercial medicine in producing a wide range of antibiotic and other substances, this is a much prized plant which flowers for a full season. Melilot is highly attractive to bees as it produces a large quantity of sweet nectar, a quality underlined by its botanical name, which means honey lotus. This yellow sweet clover bears small yellow honey-scented flowers. It flavours cheese and tobacco and was used until recently in the brewing industry. When dried, the plant has the smell of newly mown hay and for this reason was widely used to strew floors to keep them clean and fresh.

Mints

(Mentha spp.) (P) 1m, 3ft.

> *I shall never lack a good supply of common mint, in all its many varieties, all its colours, all its virtues. But if any man can name the full list of all the kinds and all the properties of mint, he must know how many sparks Vulcan sees fly into the air from his vast furnace beneath Etna.*
> WALAFRID STRABO The Little Garden 840 AD

Gone are the days when any self-respecting gardener would dismiss a bunch of mint growing in a hidden corner of his garden. Nowadays, with the return of interest in herb growing and all sweetly fragrant plants, they are more likely to spend time extolling the virtues of the twenty varieties under cultivation. As Walafrid Strabo pointed out over a thousand years ago, it is very difficult to distinguish one from another.

However, here are a few which herb growers agree about:

Eau-de-Cologne Mint, (× *piperita citrata*) is fragrant and useful for cosmetics and pot pourri. Peppermint (*Mentha piperita*) is one used to flavour

bulls-eyes and cure indigestion, some also claim it cures colds. Include this in your wine cups, pot pourris and in any cosmetics you make. Some believe its scent is better than its flavour but peppermint makes excellent tea taken hot in winter and chilled in summer.

Bowles mint (*Mentha rotundiflora* 'Bowles Variety') is for the gourmet cook. It has a delicious fruity taste, not at all without pungence and is easily identified by its thick woolly leaves which are almost round and up to three inches long, and greyish-green in colour.

Spearmint (*Mentha spicata*) is usually found in English gardens and is associated fondly with lamb and green peas. It is a light green plant, with small, pinkish flowers and the finely pointed leaves have definite toothed edges.

Apple mint creates most confusion, and botanical experts seem to disagree on the labelling of this plant. It has the scent of ripe apples overlain with traditional mint aroma, but is not as highly thought of as Bowles mint. In variegated form, the leaves are dappled with cream and white and are a most decorative addition to any garden.

Horse mint (*Mentha*

60

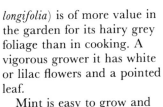

longifolia) is of more value in the garden for its hairy grey foliage than in cooking. A vigorous grower it has white or lilac flowers and a pointed leaf.

Mint is easy to grow and once established is apt to spread beyond its allotted home. Choose a mint you like and start if off from a little piece of root or keep a sprig in a jar of water until roots develop.

61

Mistletoe

(Viscum album) (P) 1m, 3ft

Mistletoe has been shrouded
in mystery for centuries. It is
classified as a herb but is
semi-parasitic and grows by

pushing its roots into the tissues of its host, usually an apple tree. The herb was highly prized by the Druids who considered the plant to possess magical qualities particularly if it was found growing on, what was to them, the sacred oak. In the past it has been associated with cures for epilepsy, convulsions and disorders of the nervous system.

The tradition of kissing under the mistletoe stems from a Scandinavian legend that Balder, the god of peace, was slain with an arrow made of mistletoe. He was restored to life at the request of the other gods and goddesses, and the herb was protected by the goddess of love. It was ordained that everyone who passed under a branch should receive a kiss, to show that mistletoe had become an emblem of love.

Motherwort

(Leonurus cardiaca) (P) 1m, 3ft

A herb known to have calming qualities, it gained its name from being used by the ancient Greeks to treat pregnant women for anxiety. The botanical name comes from the plant's resemblance to a lion's tail and its association with the heart. The herb is still in use mainly, as expressed by one old herbalist, 'to drive melancholy vapours from the heart, to strengthen it and make the mind cheerful, blithe and merry' The strong smelling herb self-seeds easily or may be propagated by root division.

Myrtle

(Myrtus communis) (P) 2m, 6ft

When dried, the green aromatic leaves of this evergreen shrub are a valuable addition to pot pourri; and when fresh one or two laid on a piece of roast meat just before it is removed from the oven will make the dish especially mouthwatering. The herb's main needs are a sheltered site on a south wall, and well drained soil. The white blossoms of the less hardy double flowered myrtle *(Myrtus Communis Flore Pleno)* are extremely fragrant.

Mullein

(Verbascum thapsus) (B) 2m, 6ft

A country name for this useful
and decorative herb is Aaron's
rod, in reference to the way
the spire-like stems with their
bright yellow flowers reach
high over other plants. The
large leaves have given it the
names donkey's ears and bull's
ears in some districts. Yet one
more name is hag's taper, for
in the days of magic and
witchcraft the dried stems
were dipped in tallow or pork
fat and used as large
firebrands to illuminate
nocturnal proceedings. The
flowers produce a yellow dye
and the leaves can be included
in a herbal smoking fixative.
Propagation is by seed sown in
the spring.

Mugwort

(Artemisia vulgaris) (P) 1.5m,
5ft

> *And if a Footman take
> Mugwort and put it into his*

mullein
myrtle

Shoes in the Morning, he may goe forty miles before Noon and not be weary.
WILLIAM COLES The Art of Simpling 1656

Mugwort has a long history; it was one of the nine herbs used to repel demons in pre-Christian times and as an ancient magical plant was known for centuries as the mother of herbs. The name derives from the old Saxon spelling meaning midge plant, since it was a much respected insect repellent. Reputedly John the Baptist wore a girdle of mugwort in the wilderness; hence the belief that it preserved wayfarers from fatigue, sun stroke, wild beasts and evil spirits. A sprig was worn on St John's Eve to protect the wearer from evil. It was used extensively to flavour drinks, particularly beer, before the introduction of hops and for many years it was made into a tea and used as a stuffing for goose.

nasturtium
nettle

Nasturtium

(Tropaelum majus) (A) Trailing

The humble but cheerful nasturtium is rarely given the credit it deserves. The slightly peppery leaves, which are rich in vitamin C, are normally picked fresh and chopped or torn for salads. Alternatively, fill the trumpets of freshly picked blooms with soft cheese, Harvest seeds while still green for pickling, when they can be used like capers.

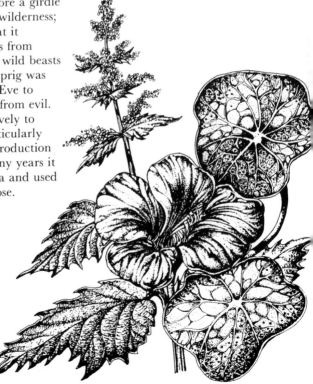

Onion

(Allium cepa) 75cm, 29in

*Onions bruised, with the
addition of a little salt, and laid
on fresh burns, draw out the
fire, and prevent the part from
blistering. Their use is fittest
for cold weather, and for aged,
phlegmatic people, whose lungs
are stuffed, and their breath
short.*

NICHOLAS CULPEPER
Complete Herbal and
English Physician ed 1826

The common onion has
been in use for so long that no
one knows where or when it
originated. The early
herbalists were aware of its use
in the treatment of coughs and
colds and through the
centuries it has been employed
for many purposes from
reducing blood pressure to
promoting the growth of hair.

A fascinating variant is the
tree onion (*Allium cepa
profilerum*), first recorded in
1587. A single bulb throws up
a hollow green stem, on top of
which a cluster of tiny onions
appear. These in turn each
throw up a stem until, finally,
the whole structure collapses.
The bulbils take root next
season and the performance
begins again.

Parsley

(Petroselinum crispum) (B)
20cm, 9in

Some people are able to grow parsley, others are not. And from this springs various beliefs about the plant thriving only where the woman 'wears the trousers' and that its roots need to go nine times down to the devil before the seedlings appear. Some poor souls, desperate to succeed, pour boiling water into the furrows in which the seed is to be sown in the hope of providing a warm, comfortable bed. Others, when presented with seedlings, heed reports that transplanted parsley brings bad luck to a garden.

There are no secrets about growing this most useful and decorative herb, but there are rules. Firstly, buy packeted seed only from a nursery or grower you can trust. Secondly make a narrow, half inch deep slit in the ground and let the sun warm it for an hour. Thirdly, sprinkle your seed lightly into the split, pull the soil back over and give the area a good soaking. For transplanting, sprinkle parsley seeds into compost you are using to put up houseplants, and seedlings will soon emerge to be pricked out when large enough to handle.

In addition to the well known Curled Parsley, nurserymen will normally supply two other varieties. These are French parsley (*Carum petroselinum*) and Hamburg parsley (*Carum petroselinum tuberosum*). The former is plain leaved and more strongly flavoured while the latter is grown for its edible root. Curled and French parsley thrive in trays, pots and tubs, provided you use good compost and prevent it from drying out. Parsley always needs to be cut back frequently, otherwise it will bolt and coarsen.

Pellitory

(Parietaria diffusa) (P) 15cm,
6in

As its name suggests, this shy
but attractive little herb is
often to be found growing
around ruins and on ancient
walls. It has been out of
fashion for many years, but
centuries ago herbalists
appreciated the plant's flavour
and used its store of potassium
salts to treat urinary
complaints. The plant has
reddish spreading stems, soft
hairy leaves and flowers like
houseleek in colour. It will
thrive if pushed into wall
crevices with a spoonful or
two of peat.

Pennyroyal

(Mentha pulegium) (P) 30cm
12in

> 'Tis good for Coughs, for the
> Gripes, the Stone, Jaundice and
> Dropsie. A spoonful of the juice
> given to Children is an excellent
> remedy for the Chin-cough
> [whooping cough] ... The
> fresh Herb wrap't in a Cloth,
> and laid in a Bed, drives away
> Fleas; but it must be renewed
> once a week.
>
> JOHN PECHEY The Compleat
> Herbal of Physical Plants
> 1694

Pennyroyal, also called
pudding grass, is now much
used by knowledgeable
gardeners and housewives as a
natural insect repellent yet its
scent is most attractive to
humans. There is a prostrate
variety which is ideal for lawn

making or for planting between paving stones. The original black puddings contained this pungent member of the mint family, and cuttings of the plant were introduced to the New World by the pilgrim fathers as a tea to induce a relaxed sleep. Its leaves, thrown into bath water, have a stimulating effect on the whole system.

Corsican mint (*Mentha requienii*) also called Spanish mint is another *habitué* of paving stones and loves being walked upon. Regarded as the smallest flowering plant grown in this country, it produces a pleasing and distinctive aroma and is ideal for planting in tubs.

Periwinkle

(Vinca major) (P) trailing

The trailing evergreen with its large fine-lobed leaves and flowers varying in colour from pale blue to purplish was highly thought of by our forefathers as a cure for many problems including nervous conditions and hypertension. It makes an attractive ground cover for shady places and is propagated by stem cuttings.

periwinkle
pimpernel

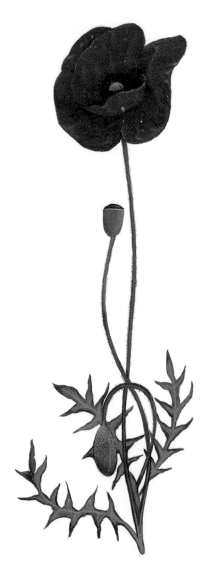

Poppy

(Papaver rhoeas) (A) 1m, 3ft

Since antiquity the poppy has featured in the imagery of sleep and oblivion, and is symbolic of the fallen in the two World Wars. An old English custom was to mix the crushed seeds of the red corn poppy with bread which is then boiled and softened in milk to induce sleep in children.

The opium poppy (*P. somniferum*) is the source of opium, morphine and heroine, both the saviour and curse of mankind. The ancient Greeks used the seeds to relieve pain and procure sleep, and since they regarded sleep as the greatest of all physicians, they crowned their nocturnal gods with wreathes of poppy blooms. In Greek mythology, the poppy was dedicated to Mix, goddess of night; to Thanatos, god of death; to Hypnos, god of sleep and to Morpheus, god of dreams.

Primrose

(Primula vulgaris) (P) 15cm, 6in

Primrose, first-born child of Ver,
Merry springtime's harbinger
The Two Noble Kinsmen

How better to describe a herb than these few lines by Shakespeare? Ver means the start of the year, when all is green. Here is another phrase:

And in the wood where often
you and I upon faint

primrose-beds were wont to lie
A Midsummer Night's Dream

As a wild plant, the delicate pale yellow petals were candied, the crinkly green leaves used in salad and the root infused as a tea to be taken in times of anxiety. Gerard, the famous herbalist, wrote in 1633 that Primrose tea 'drunk in the month of May is famous for curing phrensie'. In the past, the flowers were included in a nourishing dish called primrose pottage.

purslane
pyrethrum
ragwort

Purslane

(Portulaca oleracea) (A) trailing

A pleasant trailing salad herb with rosettes of thick, fleshy leaves which are beneficial for the blood, purslane has been popular for centuries. The ancients believed it possessed properties which counteracted magic and used it as a 'sure cure for blasting received from lightening or planets'. Those with a fear of evil spirits strewed the leaves around their beds. Most of the old recipes refer to the herb's power to cool down the system. It is propagated by sowing seeds throughout the growing season.

Pyrethrum

(Chrysanthemum cinerariifolium) (P) 30cm, 12in

A pretty white flowering herb easily confused with alecost and feverfew, pyrethrum yields what has now become the best natural insecticide. It is a native of Yugoslavia but seeds are often available for sowing in the autumn to be thinned out in the spring.

Ragwort

(Senecio jacobaea) 80cm, 30in

In folk medicine, golden ragwort was used to help reduce inflammations of the eye and as a poultice. Settlers in the New World called it female regular and squaw weed, since the American Indian women infused it as a tea to ease complications during childbirth. The golden yellow flowers can still be seen in most meadows, but they are not loved by farmers as the herb is thought to poison cattle.

Rose

(Rosa arvensis) (P) 2m, 6ft

> *Come, sit thee down upon this flow'ry bed,*
> *While I thy amiable cheeks do coy,*
> *And stick musk-roses in they sleek smooth head.*
> A Midsummer Night's Dream

Herb lovers on the trail of Shakespeare's musk-rose are now convinced that it is the trailing rose *(R. arvensis)* which blooms in midsummer and has a delicious fragrance. The

73

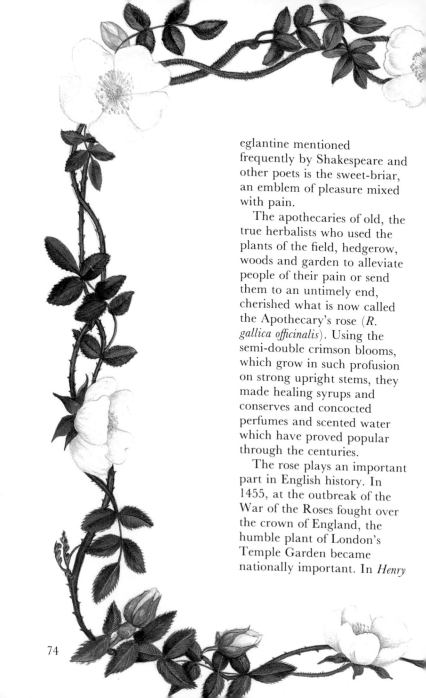

eglantine mentioned
frequently by Shakespeare and
other poets is the sweet-briar,
an emblem of pleasure mixed
with pain.

The apothecaries of old, the
true herbalists who used the
plants of the field, hedgerow,
woods and garden to alleviate
people of their pain or send
them to an untimely end,
cherished what is now called
the Apothecary's rose (*R.
gallica officinalis*). Using the
semi-double crimson blooms,
which grow in such profusion
on strong upright stems, they
made healing syrups and
conserves and concocted
perfumes and scented water
which have proved popular
through the centuries.

The rose plays an important
part in English history. In
1455, at the outbreak of the
War of the Roses fought over
the crown of England, the
humble plant of London's
Temple Garden became
nationally important. In *Henry*

VI, Part I, Richard Plantagenet of the House of York, plucked a bloom saying:

> *Let him that is a true-born gentleman*
> *And stands upon the honour of his birth*
> *If he supposes that I have pleaded truth,*
> *From off this brier pluck a white rose with me*

The Earl of Somerset took a bloom from another bush and replied:

> *Let him that is no coward and no flatterer,*
> *Pluck a red rose from off this thorn with me*

The symbolism of the action was observed by the Earl of Warwick who fatefully predicted:

> *And here I prophesy; this brawl today*
> *Grown to this faction in the Temple garden*
> *Shall send between the red rose and the white*

> *A thousand souls to death and deadly night*

Thirty-two years later, the two roses were joined in the symbolic Tudor rose.

Rosemary

(Rosmarinus officinalis) (P)
1.8m, 5ft

> *Seethe much Rosemary, and bathe therein to make thee lusty, lively, joyfull, likeing and youngly*
> WILLIAM LANGHAM The Garden of Health 1597

> *As for Rosemarine, I lett it runne all over my garden walks, not onlie because my bees love it, but because it is the herb sacred to rememberance, and therefore, to friendship; whence a sprig of it hath language that maketh it the chosen emblem of our funeral wakes.*
> SIR THOMAS MORE

Rosemary, like many old herbs, is steeped in folklore. This useful and decorative evergreen herb with misty-blue flowers is said only to flourish in the gardens of the righteous and where the wife orders the household. As its botanical name implies, it conveys images of sea spray and rocky shores as it originated among the barren cliffs of Sicily. It has established itself well in country gardens and because of its flavour was cherished by the Elizabethans. Its main enemies are frost and heavy snow, which turn the spiky leaves brown and break the branches. Rosemary is a principal herb in the composition of tussie mussies, fragrant posies still carried on certain state occasions, and is used in herbal hair rinses, bath bags, pot pourri and other natural beauty preparations. It is, however, in the kitchen that the plant enjoys its finest hours. It has numerous uses but it is particularly mouthwatering to insert sprigs of rosemary under the skin of a joint of lamb before roasting or use sprigs as a basting tool to give extra flavour to steaks and sausages.

Rosemary is propagated easily from cuttings, which grow in a few years to fragrant woody bushes.

rosemary
rue

Rue

(Ruta graveolens) (P) 1m, 3ft

An evergreen bush, though some gardeners call it 'everblue', Rue is grown now for its attractive foliage and used in historic associations. From earliest times, the strong smelling and bitter tasting herb was used as an antidote against poison. Legend relates that it protected Ulysses when his men were turned to swine.

Sage

(Salvia officinalis) (P) 50cm
20in

> *Of all garden herbes, none is of greater vertue than Sage ... such is the virtue of Sage that if it were possible, it would make up a man immortall.*
> THOMAS COGHAN The Haven of Health 1584

This great culinary herbs, was the chief medicinal herb in the Middle Ages, renowned for regenerating blood in the body and prolonging life.

The herb itself is a tough evergreen which grows in an untidy fashion on a woody stem. The broad greyish-green leaves have no accompanying flower but bright blue blooms are to be found on the attractive narrow–leaved variety. There is a purple-leaved sage, used traditionally by butchers for sausage making, and the decorative and highly aromatic pineapple sage.

Because of its reputation for prolonging life, sage is a favourite herb with those seeking good health and many opt for a daily ration by making an infusion of fresh or dried sage leaves.

Romans and Greeks believed that the plant would prosper if stolen from a neighbour's garden and that arrows rubbed with rue would find their mark. Because of this, first users of gunpowder boiled their shot in water containing the herb. The deeply cut leaves are the symbol for the suit of clubs in playing cards. A strong antiseptic, rue was used for many years in an attempt to combat the plague; in 1760, when a plague rumour swept London, the price rose by nearly fifty per cent.

Soapwort

(*Saponaria officinalis*) (P) 1m, 3ft

Fullers, the textile experts who cleaned and thickened cloth, used this hardy herb as a cleaning agent and it was described under its present name as early as 1548. Also called bouncing bet because of its habit of waving in the breeze, it is now coming back into its own as a gentle cleaner of old and delicate tapestries, a role it held in the Middle Ages and earlier. It was one of the few lathers employed to wash the famous white kid gloves of the dandies. At one time, soapwort was used as a fish poison. The plant produces clusters of pink and whitish flowers while the leaves and stem are tinted with red. It does well in poor soil and is increased by seed and root division.

Solomon's Seal

(*Polygonatum multiflorum*) (P) 50cm, 20in

The roots of Solomon's Seal, stamped while it is fresh and greene and applied, taketh away in one night or two at the most, any bruise, blacke or blew spots gotten by fals or women's wilfulness in stumbling upin their hastie husband's fists, or such like.
GERARD 1633

This very hardy herb resembles an overgrown lily of the valley and is a close relative. It was in the past to be found in virtually every cottage garden and had one special virtue in being able to reduce tell-tale or troublesome black-eyes—one old recipe called for the leaves to be beaten into a stiff ointment with lard. The herb was

*Solomon's seal
summer savory*

highly regarded as a means of mending broken bones, a decoction of roots being taken with wine. The plant was also well regarded as a cosmetic. The Italians were reported to use the distilled water of the plant for washing, a practice which was highly recommended. The herbalist Nicholas Culpeper declared that:

> *the diluted water of the whole plant used on the face or other parts of the skin, cleanses it from freckles, spots or any marks whatever, leaving the place fresh, fair and lovely for which purpose it is much used by the Italian ladies and is the principal ingredient of most of the cosmetics and beauty washes advertised by perfumers at high price.*

Summer Savory

(Satureja hortensis) (A) 30cm, 1ft

> *The leaves and flowers applied unto the head in forme of a cappe or garland, doth awake the drowsily inclined. Both thyme and winter savorie are good for the nourishing of bees, and for preserving.*
> RICHARD SURFLEET The Countrie Farme 1600

79

culinary herbs.

Speedwell

(Veronica officinalis) (P) 40cm, 16in

This is named botanically after St Veronica, who wiped Christ's face with her kerchief. The suffering features were imprinted on the cloth, making the true image. Blood, dropped on to nearby flowers which took the name veronica.

Sunflower

(Helianthus annuus) (A) 4m, 13ft

The herb has not just a pretty face for its seeds produce an oil used as a substitute for ground nut oil, widely used in foodstuffs, cosmetics and dye-making. The stems contain a fibre once used in commercial papermaking, which is still employed by specialists making the handwoven grade. The pith of the stalk is one of the lightest substances known and has helped revolutionize the design of life-saving appliances. The stalks when dry are hard as wood and make an excellent

speedwell

The peppery flavour of savory has been appreciated for centuries and the large leaves are popular as a salad, for seasoning poultry, stuffing fish and to increase the flavour of beans. The smaller leaved winter savory (*S. montana*) is a perennial propagated from cuttings or by root division. This variety is generally more useful. Once established, cut back early each spring and it will usually keep green through the year. It grows well on a window-sill or in window-box and can be planted in pots with other fire. The ash, full of potash, makes a first class manure. The buds, before fully opened, may be boiled and served like artichokes. The seeds, browned first in the oven, were once chewed to help relieve whooping cough. In country districts, some poultry keepers grow the herb in abundance as the seed is known to increase 'laying power'.

Sweet Cicily

(Myrrhis odorata) (P) 1m, 3ft

A good friend to weight watchers, this fragrant plant imparts a delicate anise flavour to food, counteracts any acidity in fruit and lessens the necessity for sugar. The large fern–like leaves, covered with fine down, are delicious just picked and eaten, and excellent for indigestion. An attractive slow-growing garden plant, reaching quite a height with tiny white flowers appearing in the late spring, it graces any garden or border. The sharply ridged black seeds are one of the ingredients of Chartreuse and have been used to perfume furniture polish. Propagation is by seed sowing and root division.

Tansy

(*Tanacetum vulgare*) (P) 60cm, 23in

> *I have heard that if maids will take wild Tansy and lay it to soake in Buttermilk for the space of nine days and wash their faces therewith, it will make them look very faire.*
> JHEROM BRUYNSWYKE The vertuouse boke Of Distyllacyon 1527

The beauty of this ancient plant lies in the long lasting knots of golden flowers which can be dried and are perfect for flower arrangers and makers of pot-pourri.

Tarragon

(*Artemisia dracunculus*) (P) 40cm, 16in

There is French tarragon and Russian tarragon, and although they look alike, only the former is of value as a culinary herb. Its underground runners, which need to be kept in check, throw up branching stems with insignificant flowers. A small piece of the runner, planted in sandy or peaty soil in a sunny position, will keep a family supplied with the herb for years. Provided it can be sprayed with water each week and given good drainage, it will grow well in a pot in a sunny corner. The leaves of tarragon may be picked fresh throughout the summer or they may be dried in trays and then stored in airtight containers for the winter. Highly regarded by keen cooks, tarragon is famous for its vinegar and as an ingredient of many famous sauces, soups and chicken dishes.

tansy

82

tarragon

Tarragon Vinegar

Place a quantity of freshly pickled clean tarragon leaves in a wide-mouthed bottle or jar. Fill the bottle with white wine vinegar and cover tightly. Keep in a sunny place for two weeks, shaking the container vigorously every day. Discard the herb and allow the liquid to strain completely through muslin into bottles with tight fitting cork or plastic lids (not metal). Before sealing, add a sprig of fresh tarragon to each bottle.

It is wise to use Tarragon sparingly. According to an old rhyme:

There are certain people
Whom certain herbs
The good digestion disturbs.
Henry the Eighth divorced
Catherine of Aragon
For her reckless use of tarragon.

Thistle

(Silybum marianum) (P) 1m, 3ft

The milk thistle is also called Marion thistle from the story that the milk of the Virgin fell upon the herb, resulting in the white veins of the leaves. This tall, extremely attractive plant, often found growing wild near old buildings, was once cultivated. The roots were regarded as great delicacies and they were sometimes baked in pies. The young leaves of the milk thistle were eaten as a cure for snakebites and for liver problems. To attract goldfinches, who love the seeds, grow some in a garden tub or in the border.

Thyme, Lemon

(Thymus x citriodorus) (P) 15cm–40cm, 6–16in

Unless you are careful, you can lose your way among

83

members of the Thyme family. Study them if you wish, and even plant a special garden of the many varieties, but for the time being, stick to the exquisitely fragrant lemon thyme for personal care and the robustly scented common garden thyme for cooking. All the thymes can be propagated easily by root division or cuttings. Common thyme, the variety most often to be found in the herb garden, will grow into a tiny ball-shaped bush within a few months if left untrimmed. The aroma of the tiny dark green leaves is particulary noticeable when they are brushed against. In summer, the plant produces a mass of sweet scented mauve flowers which are soon alive with busy bees.

The lemon thyme plant is generally neater and the leaves, giving out a delightful lemon scent, are of a richer green. It makes a useful low-growing hedge and is often planted as aromatic* ground cover around roses. Mature plants, not required for the house, may be buried up to their topmost leaves in early spring and kept well watered for a few weeks. When lifted, each of the tiny leaf–carrying branches will have thrown out shoots. If

thyme

broken off with care, these branches may be planted out and will soon mature.

According to old and new cookery books alike there are numerous dishes which will benefit from thyme. It compliments vegetables and the natural flavours of all cooked meat, tomato and cheese dishes and is used in stuffings, soups, stews and butters. Thyme made as a tea is a good mouthwash and also helps ease the miseries of colds, catarrh and throat infections. The scent is usually regarded as being too powerful for beauty preparations but the dried herb is useful in pot-pourri and sleep pillows.

Toadflax

(Linaria vulgaris) (P) 60cm, 23in

The primrose-yellow spikes and orange flowers with fleshy blue leaves have earned this little herb the country names of butter-and-eggs and eggs-and-bacon. The proper name stems from the flower's likeness to the reptile's wide mouth and also from the superstition that toads sheltered from magicians among the leaves. In summer, the herb is sometimes mistaken for flax. Both cattle and flies leave this bitter herb alone. As a repellent, boil the whole herb in milk and stand the infusion in a wide-mouthed jar where flying insects are a nuisance.

Valerian

(Valeriana officinalis) (P) 1m, 3ft

Valerian has been used for centuries to calm the nerves and give gentle sleep to those suffering too much strain. It produces clusters of pale pink flowers which attract the bees and butterflies. The plant is of great beauty but the aroma is not to everyone's liking. The thick underground runners need space to spread and given this condition it may be planted anywhere. To make a stress-relieving infusion, boil two cups of milk and pour this into a jug containing three teaspoons of fresh valerian leaves. Let the mixture steep for 5 minutes then strain it and add a tablespoon of honey, a tablespoon of vodka and a teaspoon of cider and vinegar.

Vervain

(Verbena officinalis) (P) 15cm, 6in

A handsome herb with well cut dark green leaves with pale blue flowers on a straight stalk, vervain is a herb of ancient magic. If you are superstitious, you will wear a sprig to protect you from the evil eye. Infants wearing it were believed to learn their lessons more quickly and to be of a joyful disposition. Old wives tales abound; in mediaeval times it was even suggested that a leaf pressed into a cut in the hand would help a thief open locks. The herb is remarkably easy to grow from seed and does best in an open, sunny position.

Violet

(Viola odorata) (P) 15cm, 6in

There are many forms of violet but all have come from the sweet violet which can be found growing in the hedgerows and around woodland trees. Their nodding heads have uplifted hearts for centuries. Napoleon associated them with his wife Josephine and it was later adopted as the emblem of the Imperial Napoleonic party. The ancient Greeks used the violet to moderate anger, while the ancient Britons argued that the herb, steeped in goat's milk and rubbed into the skin, increased female beauty. The nectar-laden flowers are ideal for bees while some butterflies rely on it as a source of nutrition. Today we think of the violet as being blue, but other colours have been popular.

Woodruff

(Asperula odorata) (P) 15cm, 6in

Woodruff is justly famous for the flavour and fragrance it gives to wine cups, but there are many other ways of appreciating the virtues of this tiny, almost insignificant herb once you can track it down to its hideaway beneath a tree or bush. The plant is low-growing and creeping by nature, and is best propagated by pulling it up and cutting it into root–bearing strips. Although it appreciates shade, it will spread along paving stones and grow well in window boxes. Woodruff leaves can be used fresh, but only when dried do they give out their special aroma of newly-mown hay.

National Trust
Herb Gardens to Visit

Acorn Bank
Cumbria

Bateman's
East Sussex

Castle Drogo
Devon

East Riddlesden Hall
West Yorkshire

Felbrigg Hall
Norfolk

Gunby Hall
Lincolnshire

Hardwick Hall
Derbyshire

Little Moreton Hall
Cheshire

Melford Hall
Suffolk

Moseley Old Hall
Staffordshire

St Michael's Mount
Cornwall

Scotney Castle Garden
Kent

Snowshill Manor
Gloucestershire

Springhill
County Londonderry

Wallington
Northumberland

Westbury Court Garden
Gloucestershire